AF730863

What Our Readers Have Said...

Applicability

"These books are great tools that should be used as guidelines for our everyday supervisory practices. You need to take the time to do a short self-evaluation when reading them."

•

"The things and problems we deal with everyday are discussed in these books."

•

Convenience

"I like this because I can take them with me to read at a convenient time. I feel the little time I have to spend in the office is best use on activities that directly relate to revenue opportunities. I like the short amount of time it takes to keep up with these."

•

"I just read each book, and then file it for future reference."

•

"I like the fact that the format allows the books to be reviewed as time permits. All work has been conducted on personal, evening/weekend time."

•

Challenge

"My thought is that the real value of these books comes into effect when doing the action plans."

•

"The challenge when I think a specific topic does not apply is to find a way to make it apply."

•

Clarity

"Short and sweet. These books are easy to comprehend."

•

"These books are very easy to read and clearly outlined."

•

"Easy to use, understand, and reference if needed."

•

Relevance

"I have enjoyed reading these books. They are relevant to today's work environment and the ongoing change in the way we manage our workforce."

•

"I believe the contents of the Pinpoint series are excellent. It causes one to reflect on the daily dynamics in working with oneself as well as with management and peers."

•

"I do feel that these books have been very helpful to me at my job."

•

"I do enjoy reading each of theses books and it gives some real thought to its instruction."

•

Customer Service Representative's Roles & Responsibilities

Pinpoint Customer Service Skill Development Training Series

TIMOTHY F. BEDNARZ

MAJORIUM
BUSINESS PRESS

Pinpoint Customer Service Skill Development Training Series
"Customer Service Representative's Roles & Responsibilities"
Timothy F. Bednarz

Graphic design: Monika Pawlak

Majorium Business Press
2025 Main Street
Stevens Point, WI 54481
715.342.1018 • 800.654.4935

ISBN 978-1-882181-56-8

Printed in the United States of America

Introduction

The Pinpoint Customer Service Skill Development Training Series is designed for targeted training and education regarding increased improvement in a specific skill or competency.

Each book within this series is designed to be easy to use, understand and apply to your job. It can be used as a basis for training individuals, as a discussion guide or as a personal training tool.

Each chapter within this book discusses a specific concept. When you have completed all eight chapters you should have a 360º perspective of the topic.

Additionally, each chapter is divided into specific sections:

- The first section provides you with an overview of the topic
- The Implications section discusses why the concept is important, and why it is important to learn and apply.
- The Strategies, Tips & Techniques to Apply section teaches how to use and apply the particular concept to your work.
- The Points to Ponder section gives you something to think about or to be discussed with a group setting. These are questions not meant to be immediately answered, but to be pondered over time.
- The Training Activity section provides you with the tools to transfer what you have learned to your job. It is designed to help create an action plan to effectively apply the concept.

Each of the topics in this series is time-tested and proven in the marketplace. They have been used by thousands of employees as training tools. Many of the users have commented that what made these books valuable, was the ability to refer to them when a problem surfaced. They indicated that they remembered reading about the exact problem. They referred back to these books and found an appropriate solution.

You will find them equally valuable as a resource in your professional development library.

Table of Contents

LEARNING OBJECTIVES:

- The value of quality customer service.
- To understand their role in delivering quality customer service.
- To understand their impact on the customer.
- To gain insight of what is expected of them.
- To develop the skills and knowledge required of them.
- How to handle the negative aspects of their positions.

1

The Lifelong Value of the Customer

Many service representatives view their customers as just another problem or complaint. The entire service experience is depersonalized by these attitudes. What many fail to realize is that customers are business assets and need to be viewed as such.

Due to the overwhelming number of calls received by customer service departments, it is relatively easy to become desensitized and begin to view each customer as a number. The problem occurs when this attitude is clearly conveyed to the customer. They become irritated by the fact that the representative clearly has no empathy and regard for their situation and obviously does not value their business.

When people have spent money on a product or service and a problem arises, they expect that it will be solved, and solved *fast.* They don't care that the service representative has heard it all before. They *do* care that they have spent money out of their budget, that what they have purchased is not performing as it should, and that as such, they need *service.*

IMPLICATIONS — WHAT THIS MEANS TO YOU

It is service representatives' responsibility to treat the customer with empathy, compassion and respect. The customer represents a concrete value to the company and should be dealt with accordingly. Too often service representatives think they can treat their customers poorly because there are more to replace them. Companies are learning that viewing customers as an inexhaustible resource is a mistake with dire consequences.

STRATEGIES, TIPS & TECHNIQUES TO APPLY

Customers are business assets, plain and simple. They represent a financial value to the company, yet, amazingly, all too often they have to fight for even the smallest modicum of respect from their service representative.

Stew Leonard's is a Connecticut chain of dairy stores with annual sales in excess of $100 million. Through research the company discovered that their typical customer visited one of their stores twice a week and spent an average of $50 per visit. In that area of Connecticut, the average resident stayed in the area for 10 years. Thus the company discovered the average customer was worth a hefty $50,000. As such, employees were taught to value each customer as a business asset worth $50,000. The result was that customers reciprocated with unparalleled loyalty.

Loyal customers are invaluable business assets that are often undervalued by companies. They do not only represent a base of sales: their word of mouth builds the business and supplies them with new customers. They often take a further active interest in the company, supplying ideas and suggestions that help the company improve their products and services. Unfortunately many companies view customer attrition as normal and allow valuable business assets to walk away without a fight. Research clearly demonstrates that it costs five times as much to win a new customer as it does to retain a current client. In fact Harvard Business School reported that if a company can retain the 2% of customers that companies attribute to normal attrition, it amounts to a 10% savings in operating expenses—a substantial increase in profit.

It should be noted that good service isn't enough. AT&T reported that 10% of customers who rate their service as "good" will not repurchase their services.

Customer service representatives may review these statistics and decide they do not apply to them and that they are instead an issue for management to mull over. But this is far from the case: it is within the power of each service representative to provide customer care that is average, good or exceptional. It is within the power of every service representative to recognize each customer for what he or she actually is: a business asset, rather than just another complaint or number.

Service is not a policy or department. It is an individual experience between the customer and the company representative. It involves a service attitude of empathy, respect, and the desire to be pleasant and responsive. When representatives understand the financial value each customer represents, it is easier to truly be of service to them.

POINTS TO PONDER — SOMETHING TO THINK ABOUT

1. Have you considered your customers to be business assets?
2. Does seeing each of your customers as an asset change how you view them?

TRAINING ACTIVITY — APPLICATION & ACTION PLAN

Calculate the lifetime value of your customers.

1. Determine the average purchase.
2. Identify the frequency of the purchases.
3. Determine how long the average customer remains with the company.
4. Calculate their value to your company.

2

The Consequences of Poor Customer Service

The poor attitude of one uncaring service representative can cause a chain reaction with consequences rippling to every corner of the organization. Without the intervention of management to resolve the problem and correct future actions, it can have disastrous consequences for a company.

In a properly managed setting the careless actions of a single service representative are easily identified and corrected. The representative is then properly trained or, if all else fails, eliminated from the position. In many companies, however, such a problem may be indicative of the attitudes of the entire customer service department, their unprofessional behavior accepted and tolerated by management.

IMPLICATIONS — WHAT THIS MEANS TO YOU

How service representatives treat the individual customer does have consequences. The fact that poor service attitudes are tolerated does not make them acceptable—least of all to the paying customer. The customer always has the option to vote with their dollar and take their business elsewhere. If enough of them do so, the company will find itself in a precarious situation.

STRATEGIES, TIPS & TECHNIQUES TO APPLY

Poor customer service triggers a downward company spiral that, due to the following consequences, is extremely difficult to pull out of. It should be noted that these consequences are normally multiplied exponentially over a number of poorly treated customers. This intensifies their effect, and is where the real damage can occur.

Consequence #1

The customer leaves the business dissatisfied. According to Technical Assistance Research Programs (TARP), he or she will become an "ambassador of ill will," telling a minimum of 10 people of the experience. Since, not surprisingly, people are more willing to listen to "word of mouth" recommendations than a company's advertising, over time business is substantially impacted. If the customer is sufficiently angered, he or she will actively work to damage the company's business. This can have serious repercussions.

Consequence #2

Word of mouth travels, identifying the company as a place where it is pointless to complain, as it does nothing to resolve problems to the customer's satisfaction. This will understandably deter new customers from wanting to do business with the company.

Consequence #3

Once clients stop complaining and vote with their feet, the company loses an essential opportunity to learn what it can do to improve its services and meet customers' needs. Complaints provide companies essential feedback regarding their products and services. This enables them to make changes and improvements that add value and increase customer satisfaction.

Consequence #4

Product and service quality are not improved. In increasingly competitive markets, product development cannot be ignored and left to languish. When it does, the product/service ultimately declines in reputation and is surpassed by superior competitive offerings.

Consequence #5

In order to remain competitive, the company is forced to reduce prices rather than add value with improved products. The customer base ultimately becomes comprised of price shoppers who have little loyalty and will readily switch for a cheaper product, regardless of quality and value. This forces the company to continually drop their prices and reduces the profits required to develop new products and services. Ultimately, other services are reduced and employees are laid off to compensate for losses.

Consequence #6

Employees do not enjoy dealing with ill-natured customers. They begin to harbor contempt and disdain for them. This attitude is readily conveyed to the customers, further eroding the value of customer service and creating additional customer dissatisfaction.

Consequence #7

Quality employees become demoralized by the situation and often seek other employment. This deprives the company of essential skills, expertise and experience required to rectify the situation. The remaining staff is less motivated and incapable of rebuilding customer trust, confidence and loyalty. This further eats away at the customer base.

Consequence #8

The increase of dissatisfied and fleeing customers reinforces the downward cycle as they transmit their experiences to the people they know. The cycle begins again, and the company's problems deepen.

Left unchecked, these eight consequences are repeated over and over again to the point that a company is unable to recover.

POINTS TO PONDER — SOMETHING TO THINK ABOUT

1. Have you considered the impact on the company of how you treat your customers?
2. Do you understand the consequences that poor service and uncaring attitudes can have on your company?

TRAINING ACTIVITY — APPLICATION & ACTION PLAN

1. Examine the eight consequences of poor service. Identify any you feel your company may be experiencing.
2. Discuss the situation with coworkers and associates and determine corrective actions.
3. Discuss your findings with your service supervisor.

3

Why Your Position Is Important

Whether or not a company is able to build loyal and long-term customer relationships depends upon the daily actions and attitudes of its customer service representatives. The position filled by every service rep is vital. By utilizing each one's capabilities and assets—including the ability to have and maintain a positive outlook—companies are able to stay closer to their customers and gain insight into future needs and interests, which is critical to meeting new market demands.

Customer service representatives alone often determine whether or not their company remains competitive, thriving and growing. The basic objective of their position is to effect positive customer encounters. These contacts can be categorized according to the impact created. In their position, service representatives are expected to provide a decidedly positive customer experience that leads each one back to the company's door.

IMPLICATIONS – WHAT THIS MEANS TO YOU

How customer service representatives personally manage their individual "moments of truth," or every contact with their customers, can either positively or negatively impact their company's financial future. Their job requires a complete understanding that each of their actions has consequences, regardless of whether they have the opportunity to interact with that individual customer again.

STRATEGIES, TIPS & TECHNIQUES TO APPLY

Customers come to a company with specific ideas and expectations of what constitutes good or exceptional service. While these are often not very demanding, it is surprising how many companies and service representatives fail to meet them. Often clients just want a simple problem solved or question answered, but are instead thoroughly irritated by a system that forces them to jump through hoops just to get a "live body." When they are finally graced with a representative, they are treated rudely and curtly.

Customer care representatives deliver exceptional service when they understand three positive outlooks that lead to positive contacts and keep customers satisfied and loyal. These constructive mindsets help assure service representatives will be successful in their jobs.

'I will get the customer's order right the first time, or, if there are problems, immediately correct them to their satisfaction'

The customer service representative who consistently gets the customer's order right or fixes a problem the first time is fulfilling his or her primary role—to deliver exceptional service. As simple as it appears, careless attitudes or apathy toward the customer is the biggest barrier to accomplishing this mission. It is a caring attitude and an accompanying attention to detail that allows service representatives to succeed.

A careless and sloppy attitude compounds problems by creating even more difficulties. A lack of attention to the little things needed to solve a problem frustrates the customer causing them to become further irritated with the system and the service representatives they have to work with. They often do not talk with the same representative more than once, so there is no accountability or concern if the problem isn't fixed right the first time. It's a problem that just gets passed along until the customer goes away or someone takes the time to fix it. In both cases the consequences are less than desirable.

Not 'What do you want,' but 'How do you want it'

Problems in personal attitudes are created when service representatives feel they must be subservient to the customer—and resent it. They feel they are the customer's servant or slave, and that they aren't paid enough to deal with other people's problems. This resentment and attitude is readily apparent in their tone and lack of civility. Rather than conducting themselves professionally, they take a "What do you want?" stance toward the customer, as though he or she is an unwelcome intrusion. The customer walks away from these individuals feeling abused, not helped. The service representative's poor behavior translates into the customer resenting ever having dealt with the company in the first place.

Each contact is an opportunity to further a client relationship through open dialogue and collaborative conversation

It takes a special person to be a successful customer service representative, one with a service attitude. This is markedly different than a servant mentality. Good representatives know they are not subservient to the customer, they just want to be of help. They don't see the customer's call as another problem, but as an opportunity to be of service.

Individuals who develop and nurture an attitude of service are less likely to burnout in the job, because they are helping the customer solve his or her problem rather than fighting and resisting their intrusions. They have compassion and empathy for the customer, knowing they themselves would want to be helped were they in their shoes. Understanding they too would be frustrated, they do everything within their power to minimize and ultimately eliminate their customer's problem.

POINTS TO PONDER — SOMETHING TO THINK ABOUT

1. Do you assume a servant mentality or service attitude as a customer service representative?
2. What personally hinders you from providing exceptional service to your customers?

TRAINING ACTIVITY — APPLICATION & ACTION PLAN

On a sheet of paper create two columns headed "Servant Mentality" and "Service Attitude."

1. List the characteristics you feel define each attitude or outlook.
2. Identify the positive and negative aspects of each characteristic both from your perspective and the customer's perspective.
3. Determine which of the two is most beneficial to you, the customer and your company.

4

The Impact on the Customer

While service representatives often begin their conversations with "How may I help you" or "How may I be of service," many fail to understand the full meaning and import of those words.

When clients spend their money on a product or service and have a problem, they have clear-cut expectations of how they should be treated. They are not a number in line or a complaint, but a paying customer. They have a basic need to feel that they are valued and important as customers. Though their problems may appear minor and irritating to the service representative, they want to be appreciated for the inconvenience the problem is causing them.

IMPLICATIONS — WHAT THIS MEANS TO YOU

Customers first and foremost want to be treated as human beings in need of assistance, not as inconveniences. They have basic requirements and expectations that they need met. Unfortunately, due to the nature of the job and the sheer number of customer contacts, many reps tend to forget this fact. Losing their service attitude and instead feeling a slave to their customers, they see each client as "another problem" or a number. They become desensitized to the personal needs of the customer.

STRATEGIES, TIPS & TECHNIQUES TO APPLY

The service representative has the singular ability to impact how the customer perceives the total value of the product or service he or she has purchased. In many cases company policies and procedures hamper his or her ability to get help with an issue.

For instance, the service representative may be talking with a customer after a prolonged wait on hold has already made them irritated. What should have been a relatively simple experience has turned into a marathon encounter. In other cases, companies force customers to hunt through their websites before calling for an answer or demand a fee for the right to talk to a service representative. What is more convenient for the company is often done at the customer's expense. Consequently, they are angry and frustrated before they even get through to a service representative.

These are hurdles the average client can be forced to overcome from the very start. Little wonder many companies receive low grades for their customer service: they make their customers work for it and not the other way around.

When viewed from that light, service representatives have to provide exceptional service just to overcome the initial negative experiences the customer was forced to endure. When service representatives respond with a curt and surly attitude to an already agitated customer, they are only fueling the customer's irritation. Not surprisingly, when customers experience this attitude, they respond negatively, resulting in the service representative becoming still more hostile towards the customer. Rather than resolving the situation, the representative is only compounding it.

However, when service representatives take the time to be more caring and concerned about the customer's experience, they can go a long way to turning a negative experience into a positive one. When they understand the customer just wants to fix an existing problem or get a question answered quickly and without a hassle, it is easy to meet these expectations.

A simple acknowledgement of the customer's problems and the hassle to get to this point often can go a long way to overcoming a negative experience. Like most people, customers want to feel important. They want the service representative to understand what they are going through and the inconvenience it has caused them. That is not an unrealistic expectation. It is surprising how smoothly things can go once representatives take the time to acknowledge the customer as a person and appreciate the difficulties they are experiencing. This simple display of empathy creates a strong and lasting impact that will win the customer over.

Once this has been accomplished, the representative should clearly and concisely explain to the customer what they plan to do for him or her. This further reinforces that they do care. If there are any possible delays, this should be explained and noted ahead of time. Representatives should indicate that they will follow up to make sure any additional delays and potential problems are overcome. This often will take an additional call or two on the representative's part to assure satisfaction.

These simple actions will create a sense of relief, surprise and appreciation for the actions of the service representative. It clearly and unmistakably communicates that he or she is genuinely concerned and understands their client's problems. Even if problems and delays occur, the customer will be more understanding and accepting of a service representative that treats them in this manner. Research has shown when people are treated with this level of care and concern they are more likely to become extremely loyal customers.

Customers just want to feel valued, important and understood. These are basic human needs that every service representative should be capable of delivering.

POINTS TO PONDER — SOMETHING TO THINK ABOUT

1. Do you understand the basic human needs each customer comes to you with?
2. Are you so overwhelmed by customer calls that you feel unable to meet their needs?

TRAINING ACTIVITY – APPLICATION & ACTION PLAN

1. Make a log of one day's service calls. Across the top of a sheet of paper list the following objectives:
    - Appreciative
    - Served
    - Valued
    - Important
    - Understood
2. After each call, note how well you did in each of the five objectives.
3. At the end of the day, review your call log and analyze the results.
4. Determine if you accomplished the five objectives consistently.
5. Identify the actions you need to take to improve your performance.
6. Once a week for thirty days, repeat this exercise.

5

Developing a Service Attitude

A service attitude is an essential prerequisite for those in the customer service profession. Many within this vocation bring an automatic desire to serve to the job. This makes it easier to fulfill their roles and responsibilities and represents a source of continual personal satisfaction.

The simple desire to be of assistance allows service representatives to see their part in their company's success as going far beyond that of a job. Exceptional customer service is delivered when representatives develop a service attitude linked with a genuine desire to help their customers.

IMPLICATIONS – WHAT THIS MEANS TO YOU

Each service representative's success is determined by their desire to be of help to their customers. Their ability to succeed and their responsibility to contribute positively to their company's success must transcend the boundaries of the job. Individuals willing to give a little bit extra to create a satisfied customer deliver exceptional service. Their personal gratification is derived from making their customers happy and knowing they did a good job.

STRATEGIES, TIPS & TECHNIQUES TO APPLY

The foundation of a service attitude is the positive personal outlook an individual brings to the job. This cannot be overemphasized because it underscores the critical importance of an exceptional service attitude. Built upon that foundation are the additional attributes of a service attitude, including:

Desire to Be of Service

An exceptional customer service representative must view their position as more than a job. They must possess the personal desire to be of help to people. Even in the business-to-business environment, the service representative is dealing with people who have the same basic needs as customers in retail. This is opposed to a "servant mentality" where representatives operate as though they are being forced to serve the customer and are demeaned by the experience. With a genuine desire to serve people, service representatives will automatically do that which is needed to help their customers—and beyond.

Desire to Produce a Positive Outcome

A service representative with a service attitude will make sure the customer's experience is not concluded until a positive outcome is achieved. They know they are not being of true service until the customer's request is fully complied with. They also understand there are limits to what they can do, and that if the customer's request exceeds those boundaries, they know where to refer them to meet their needs.

Desire to Demonstrate Care, Concern and Understanding

A service attitude goes beyond wanting to help, to include making certain the customer understands their business is valued and important. Representatives make sure the customer feels his or her problems and concerns are understood and cared about.

Service representatives who display a service attitude and apply liberal amounts of empathy and compassion also understand that they have the ability to win the customer's loyalty and ensure that the company keeps their business.

Desire to Make the Customer Happy

Representatives with a service attitude have a genuine desire to make sure the customer is happy and satisfied with the solution they were provided. If they are not, they will take the necessary steps to assure customer satisfaction, including referring the problem to a higher level when required.

Desire to Make a Positive Contribution

Exceptional service representatives fully understand the positive financial impact they can have on their company when they deliver good service to their customers. They understand the role they play in their company's success and take their responsibilities seriously. They have a sincere desire to contribute as well as to be of service.

POINTS TO PONDER — SOMETHING TO THINK ABOUT

1. Do you feel you are exhibiting a genuine service attitude in your job?
2. Do you resent your customers or do you welcome contact with them?

TRAINING ACTIVITY — APPLICATION & ACTION PLAN

1. On a sheet of paper, list the following characteristics.
    - Desire to Be of Service
    - Desire to Produce a Positive Outcome
    - Desire to Demonstrate Care, Concern and Understanding
    - Desire to Make the Customer Happy
    - Desire to Make a Positive Contribution

2. Under each list three of four things you do to fulfill each.
3. If you are unable to list things you are actually doing, list three or four things that you should be doing.

6

Developing Customer Service Skills

To be effective, customer service representatives must possess a set of essential skills and develop key areas of knowledge and expertise. Critical to their success, these are all areas that should be developed throughout the service representative's career.

Customers are becoming more demanding, requiring a proportionate increase in service representatives' skills and expertise. Representatives who fail to adapt to this changing environment will face more problems, issues and angry customers in the performance of their duties and responsibilities. It is no longer enough to be pleasant on the phone. Increasing customer demands are linked with rising expectations that service representatives are expected to meet.

IMPLICATIONS — WHAT THIS MEANS TO YOU

More is being expected of customer service representatives, and their position in most companies is rising to a level of importance equal to that of selling. The success of a company requires superior customer service, with representatives possessing critical skills to be proficient and effective in fulfilling their responsibilities.

STRATEGIES, TIPS & TECHNIQUES TO APPLY

Customer service representatives must be proficient in the four critical areas discussed below.

Technical Skills

Service representatives must develop a solid understanding of the equipment and systems they are working with. This does not require in-depth technical knowledge, but representatives should be able to respond to error messages and be versed in the correct procedures to follow if the system does go down.

Additionally, service representatives should understand the flow of and purpose behind both the paper and electronic information circulating within their organization. Since information flow affects the speed and reliability of personal attention provided to customers, service representatives must be well-versed in the proper protocols and procedures to follow. This includes knowing what happens to information and requests once they are entered into the system, as well as how to follow up and correct problems if and when they occur. As it is all too easy to "push enter and forget about it," service representatives should understand exactly what happens to information once they submit it as well as the subsequent steps to follow. They should also know where to report a system problem or breakdown so that it does not recur.

Interpersonal Skills

Service representatives should have a personal attitude focused on being of service to the customer. They should be able to listen, understand, relate to, have compassion for and empathize with their customers. Additionally, they should be able to demonstrate a thorough knowledge of their company's products and services. Ultimately, service representatives must polish their skills so that any interaction with the customer is positive and does not offend or embarrass them.

These skills are strengthened through training, knowledge and experience. Over time service representatives will develop the heightened degree of experience and expertise essential to the performance of their jobs.

Product and Service Knowledge

Service representatives should develop product and service knowledge in four basic areas:

Technical Aspects – Service representatives should be well acquainted with the technical aspects of their company's products and services. They should be proficient enough in these areas to exhibit a higher degree of product knowledge than their customers.

Competition – Service representatives should know all facts of interest to their customers regarding the competition's products and services.

FAQ's – Service representatives should be familiar with customers' most frequently asked questions and how to adequately answer them.

Needs and Expectations – Service representatives should understand and anticipate the basic needs and expectations customers have when contacting their company. They should know how to meet—and where possible, exceed—these expectations as well as understand the consequences if they fail to do so.

Customer Knowledge

Service representatives should be intimately acquainted with their customers. This includes knowing how and why they purchase the company's product(s), how they use them, and the consequences if the product or service does not perform properly or fails.

While in-depth client information is developed over time and through experience, even the most novice of service representatives should possess basic customer knowledge. It is important not only to possess this information, but also to clearly understand it and its implications when applied to daily service activities.

POINTS TO PONDER — SOMETHING TO THINK ABOUT

1. Were you aware of all the skills and knowledge service representatives must possess to be successful?
2. Can you identify areas you are weak in that have caused problems for you?

TRAINING ACTIVITY — APPLICATION & ACTION PLAN

1. Determine the depth of your skills and knowledge. On a sheet of paper, list the following items:
    - Technical Skills
    - Interpersonal Skills
    - Product and Service Knowledge
        - Technical Aspects
        - Competition
        - Frequently Asked Questions
        - Needs and Expectations
    - Customer Knowledge
2. Identify the skill level and proficiency you have attained for each area.
3. Define your strengths and weaknesses in each area.
4. Identify the areas that you need to personally develop.
5. Discuss with your manager or supervisor how you can increase your skills and knowledge in each area that you have identified.

7

What You Need to Know About Customer Service

Due to the nature of the customer service representative's role and his or her level in the company, it is easy to dismiss the importance of their work. Yet without good service representatives, any company will suffer negative marketplace effects.

Not only do customer service representatives provide an initial contact point for most customers, they are also the source of critical information that a company needs access to in order to improve and succeed. The service representative's competence in identifying sources of problems and accurately and completely recording that information in the company's informational system is critical to both their individual and corporate success.

IMPLICATIONS — WHAT THIS MEANS TO YOU

It is all too easy for service representatives to overlook the importance of accurate and detailed information and input only the minimal requirements into the system. Yet companies need service representatives who can not only successfully manage the customer relationship and resolve their problems, but who are also capable of thoroughly recording critical complaint-related information that companies can use to pinpoint trends and problems and resolve them before they turn into major public relations setbacks.

STRATEGIES, TIPS & TECHNIQUES TO APPLY

Customer service plays a pivotal role in a company's success. It provides realistic feedback that allows the company to pinpoint problems and defects in the following areas, then take corrective action so they don't recur.

Customer Problems

When companies design products and services, potential problems and flaws are anticipated. Yet, invariably, unforeseen and unanticipated glitches will arise that cause customer problems. Customer service provides a reporting mechanism not only to relate these problems and inconveniences, but also to get them resolved. In some cases the problems are minor and can be rectified with the assistance of both customer and technical service. In other cases, the problems are major and require product replacement or an on-site service call by a company representative. In all cases, it is crucial that companies have the ability to capture this information, analyze it and take action to rectify it. The customer service representative is on the front lines of this process and is the person with whom a customer will normally establish first contact.

Customer Dissatisfaction

While most customers reporting problems can accept the fact that a product or service is not perfect as long as the matter is resolved quickly, it is extremely important for companies to understand the factors that led to the service issue. These can often go beyond the initial product defect or problem to include the company's response, policies and/or implementation of service procedures once the problem has been brought to light. Part of the service representative's role is to carefully track and record each step taken in resolving the problem until the customer is satisfied. This is information that companies must have access to in order to streamline their policies and procedures and assure that customer dissatisfaction is minimized.

Product Problems

Customer problems can stem from a variety of product-related sources including missing or defective parts, poor design, inadequate/unclear instructions or improper installation. Whatever the cause, service representatives must be able to initially identify the source and refer the customer to the proper department for resolution or replacement. Within some companies, the service representative is authorized to take these actions on the customer's behalf. However, this information must be captured accurately by the service agent and inputted into the right areas of the informational system so that the company and its technical/engineering departments can assimilate the feedback they are getting from actual customer use and application.

Product Defects

The corollary to product problems is the existence of product defects. By proper tracking of the number of problems and accurately pinpointing their causes, companies can determine whether product defects do in fact exist so that the appropriate corrective actions can be taken. These may include product recalls if the problem is serious enough to cause physical harm, as well as a complete product and manufacturing review and possible redesign.

The customer service representative plays an important role in properly pinpointing product defects and reporting them so their company can take immediate action to resolve the problem. When defects do occur, they can hurt a company's reputation. The key to preventing permanent damage is quick and timely action. This is clearly seen in the case of tainted Tylenol products resulting in deaths. McNeil Pharmaceuticals immediately recalled the product from store shelves in order to prevent further harm prior to conducting an investigation. It was later discovered that an individual introduced the tainted products into a single store. However, the quick actions of the company maintained the reputation of the product and the integrity of the brand.

Customer Retention

The frontline responsibility of the customer service representative is to ensure customer retention through their actions, attitudes and timely responses.

The customer's complaint is a gift. It gives the company access to necessary and essential feedback. It also provides the opportunity to shine and prove itself to the customer. It is a pivotal "moment of truth." Despite the fact a problem arose, it is the service representative's responsibility to affirm the customer's good decision to place his or her confidence in the company's product. Properly handled, such a client can be turned into an extremely loyal customer. At this critical point, it is all in the hands of the individual customer service representative. Handled improperly, the company will permanently lose the customer and damage its reputation in the market.

POINTS TO PONDER — SOMETHING TO THINK ABOUT

1. Are you aware of the importance of your position in your company?
2. How seriously do you take the accurate and detailed recording of information regarding customer problems?

TRAINING ACTIVITY — APPLICATION & ACTION PLAN

Listed below are the five critical areas wherein customer problems develop:

- Customer Problems
- Customer Dissatisfaction
- Product Problems
- Product Defects
- Customer Retention

1. Cite a specific example of each that you have personally encountered in your company.
2. Highlight how you are able to identify each and separate one from another.
3. When encountered, detail the actions you must or are authorized to take.
4. Describe how this information is captured and reported to your company.
5. Determine ways to more accurately report the details and facts to your company.

8

The Importance of Feedback

Companies that set goals for themselves but fail to develop a competent feedback system are proceeding without a compass to keep them on track. Goals provide employees with a sense of direction; feedback tells them if they are on course. One of the primary roles of the customer service department is to capture the customer's feedback to see if they are indeed on the course that management has set.

As customer satisfaction and retention play an increasingly important role in most companies' strategies, the role of superior customer service is also ascending in importance. In the past, this area was relegated to a minor role of handling customer complaints. Managers were aware that customer service was necessary, but are only now realizing the critical role it plays in delivering and ensuring customer satisfaction.

IMPLICATIONS — WHAT THIS MEANS TO YOU

Knowledge of customer behaviors and feedback is playing an increasingly critical role in a company's ability to differentiate itself from the competition. Today, too many products are produced in a similar fashion, offering customers comparable if not the same features and benefits. People buy difference—and what is increasingly distinguishing companies is the quality of service they can deliver to their customers. Superior and sustainable service cannot be delivered without adequate feedback. This is where the importance of the service representative is elevated to a primary disseminator of the feedback they receive through constant customer contact.

STRATEGIES, TIPS & TECHNIQUES TO APPLY

Highly effective companies analyze the outcomes and processes produced by their customer service efforts. Only when both are taken into consideration can a company provide superior and sustainable levels of service that ensure both satisfaction and increased customer retention. This gives management a complete perspective of what is happening internally as well as in the marketplace.

Customer Experience

It is not enough to measure whether the customer was satisfied with the end result of their service encounter. It is also important to understand their total experience with the company. A customer may have experienced a positive outcome in that his or her problem was resolved, but if they had a difficult time obtaining that result, the net effect will be similar to that of not having had their problem solved at all.

Many companies have developed very efficient service systems that direct customers to a website to obtain assistance. The problem is, rather than getting a quick and painless answer, the customer often has to hunt for a phone number, endure long stretches of time on hold, or even pay a service fee to talk to a live representative. This adds to their frustration, fails to meet their expectations and produces a series of negative "moments of truth," or contacts with the company. While the service representative may have effectively solved the customer's problem, the string of negative experiences leading up to the solution negates their positive contribution. He or she may have done their job, but the system failed the customer.

When service representatives work within this type of environment and experience or sense overall client frustration with the system, they must capture these feelings and report them as part of the essential feedback that is crucial for management to receive. It is easy to discount these feelings and assume management is aware of the problems the system is causing and the damage the company's reputation is suffering. However, they are often entirely out of the loop unless this information is captured and reported. It is the service representative's responsibility to receive and forward this information rather than dismiss it as a customer inconvenience of little or no consequence.

Quality of Outcomes

When companies have measured the customer's total experience, they can then receive feedback from service representatives regarding the quality of the outcome the client received. The customer has an expectation of not only the experience they should have with a company, but also of the quality of the outcome. In other words, some companies and representatives will do just enough to satisfy the customer, when it only requires a little more effort to deliver complete customer satisfaction. More importantly, customer expectations are fluid and ever-changing. The only way for a company to gauge and measure these morphing customer expectations is through the feedback received from their service agents.

The service representative has a great deal of control over the quality of outcomes he or she produces for the customer. An effective representative with a true service attitude will expend a small amount of extra effort to make sure the customer is truly satisfied—and will refuse to terminate the contact until they are. On the other hand, a service representative with a resentful servant mindset will do just enough to get the job done. The outcomes may be similar, but in the latter case, the customer is left with a bittersweet taste that essentially says, "They did just enough to keep me quiet."

In both instances, the experience must be captured and reported for management to get a complete picture of what is transpiring and make the necessary adjustments in policies, training, and, where necessary, service personnel.

Service Process

The final leg of quality customer service is garnering feedback regarding the effectiveness of the entire service process. Service representatives need to capture their responses and requests for additional support within the company. Once this information is logged, the service process can be carefully monitored and tracked to ensure that there are no breakdowns that inhibit good service response and that the customer receives what is promised in a timely fashion. This information is then analyzed and correlated with the data provided through feedback on the customer experience and the quality of the outcomes.

When viewed from these three different perspectives, management can determine the overall effectiveness of their service program and how it influences the customer's commitment to keep his or her business with the company. While this is a function of management, the service representative plays an essential role by supplying accurate and detailed feedback.

POINTS TO PONDER — SOMETHING TO THINK ABOUT

1. Do you constantly observe information and feedback that you feel is important for your company to be aware of but is not captured and forwarded?
2. How carefully do you capture customer feedback? Due to the volume of calls, do you provide minimal feedback or do you take the time to accurately report it in detail?

TRAINING ACTIVITY — APPLICATION & ACTION PLAN

1. Discuss as a group the following issues:
   - The degree and detail of customer feedback that is captured and reported.
   - Information that is observed, but should be recorded.
   - Information observed that management should be aware of, but

is not reported.

- Methods to increase the value, detail and timeliness of the information captured.

2. Report and discuss your findings with your supervisors and managers.

About the Author

Timothy F. Bednarz, Ph.D. is CEO of the American Management Development Group, Inc. For over 20 years he has researched, designed and authored hundreds of learning and development programs used by Fortune 1000 companies.

He is also the author of *Great! What Makes Leaders Great. What They Did, How They Did It and What You Can Learn from It* (2011).

Speaking Availability

Timothy F. Bednarz, Ph.D. is available for speaking engagements for your next meeting or association event. He can be contacted at 800-654-4935 or by e-mail at timothy.bednarz@majorium.com.

Bulk Sales

Bulk sales of this book or any other titles available from Majorium Business Press. Inquiries can be directed to sales@majorium.com, or by phone at 800-6654-4935.

Quick Order Form

Fax orders: 715-342-1118. Send this form.

Telephone orders: Call 800-654-4935 toll-free. Have your credit card ready.

Email orders: sales@majorium.com

Postal orders: Majorium Business Press, 2025 Main Street, Stevens Point, WI 54481, USA.

Please send the following books:

____

____

____

____

Please send more FREE information on:

☐ Catalog ☐ Speaking/Seminars ☐ Mailing Lists ☐ Consulting

Name: __________________________________

Address: ________________________________

City: ____________________ State: _____ Zip: _________

Telephone: ______________________________

Email address: ___________________________

Sales tax: Please add 5.5% for products shipped to Wisconsin addresses.

Shipping by air:

United States: $4.00 for first book and $2.00 for each additional product.

International: $9.00 for first book; $5.00 for each additional product (estimate).

Made in United States
Troutdale, OR
11/03/2026

56844894R00027